BERRINGTON HALL

Herefordshire

National Trust

BERRINGTON HALL is 3 miles north of Leominster and
7 miles south of Ludlow on the west side of the A49.

Acknowledgements

This guidebook draws on the previous edition by James
Lees-Milne. I am particularly grateful to Lord Cawley for
permission to use his tape-recorded reminiscences of life at
Berrington, and for his comments on the text; also to Sir
Tatton Sykes for permission to quote from Lady Sykes's 1796
diary; and to Edward Harley for permission to reproduce the
portrait of Sarah, Lady Rodney. Chattels accepted in lieu of
Inheritance Tax by HM Government and allocated to the
National Trust, 1957, 1959 and 1961.

Oliver Garnett, 1997

Photographs: The City of London Libraries and Guildhall
Art Gallery p.37; Robert Holden Ltd/Prudence Cuming
Associates Ltd p.44; National Trust p.46; National Trust Images/
John Hammond front cover, pp.1, 5 (top and bottom), 7, 12, 14
20, 26 (bottom), 40, 41, 43, 45; NT Images/Nadia MacKenzie
pp.6, 11, 13, 18, 21, 22–23, 25, 26 (top), 27, 29, 30, back cover;
NT Images/Rupert Truman pp.4, 28, 31, 32, 33, 38, 39, 47;
NT Images/Andreas von Einsiedel pp.8–9, 16, 18, 19.

High-quality prints from the extensive and unique collections of
the National Trust Images are available at www.ntprints.com

First published in Great Britain in 1997 by the National Trust
© 1997 The National Trust
Registered charity no.205846

Revised 2000, 2003, 2004, 2009, 2010, 2011

ISBN 978-1-84359-053-8

Designed and typeset by James Shurmer (03 11)

Printed by Acorn Press for the National Trust (Enterprises) Ltd,
Heelis, Kemble Drive, Swindon, Wilts SN2 2NA
on Cocoon Silk made from 100% recycled paper

(*Front cover*) A French armchair in the Drawing Room

(*Title-page*) The Dining Room chimneypiece is decorated with
Carrara marble panels which appear to celebrate Admiral
Rodney's naval triumphs: here a man holds a crane (symbolising
valour), while at his feet is a battleship in full sail

(*Back cover*) The Drawing Room ceiling includes a central
medallion painted in the style of Biagio Rebecca, which depicts
Jupiter, Cupid and Venus

CONTENTS

BERRINGTON HALL

'A scene of elegance and refinement'

BERRINGTON was created essentially by one man, Thomas Harley, who bought the estate from the Cornewall family around 1775. He had made his fortune as a banker and government contractor in London, but had long family links with Herefordshire, to which in his mid-40s he was keen to retire from the hurly-burly of City politics.

Harley commissioned 'Capability' Brown to lay out the park, which has spectacular views west towards Wales and the Black Mountains. Around 1778 he also called in Brown's son-in-law, Henry Holland, to design him a new house in the latest French-influenced Neo-classical style, using the finest London craftsmen. The severity of the red sandstone exterior, with its gigantic Ionic portico, belies the delicacy of the interior, which contains elegant chimneypieces, plasterwork and, in the Staircase Hall, one of Holland's most sophisticated experiments in space, light and colour.

Harley had no surviving male heir, but was delighted when in 1781 his second daughter Anne married the son of Admiral Lord Rodney, one of the greatest naval commanders of the 18th century. The battle paintings in the Dining Room celebrate two of Rodney's most famous victories. On Harley's death in 1804, Berrington passed to the Rodney family, who lived here for the next 95 years. Unfortunately, George, 7th Lord Rodney

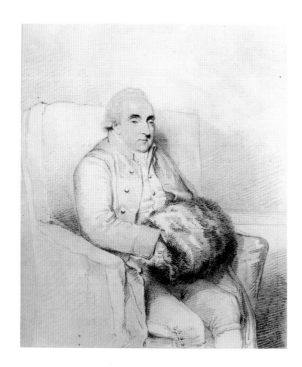

1908 with considerable sympathy, and many of his schemes still survive. He replaced ugly Victorian fire grates with more appropriate Georgian models, including those in the Drawing and Dining Rooms, but otherwise did little to disturb Holland's beautiful original design. It was in this cherished state that the house came to the National Trust in 1957, in part-payment of death-duties on the estate of the 2nd Lord Cawley, who had died three years earlier. His widow, Vivienne, Lady Cawley, generously provided an endowment and continued to live in the house until her death at the age of 100 in 1978.

By 1966 the soft stone from which the house was built had decayed so badly that the Trust was obliged to undertake an expensive four-year programme of stonework repair. After Lady Cawley's death, the house was left somewhat underfurnished, so it was particularly fortunate that in 1981 the National Trust should be bequeathed by Mrs C.V. Lawson the Elmar Digby collection of 18th-century French furniture, clocks and works of art, which now looks very much at home in the French-inspired Drawing Room and Boudoir.

In 1784 the indefatigable traveller Lord Torrington paid a visit to Berrington Hall. He found it 'gay, just finish'd and furnish'd in all the modern elegance, commanding beautiful views, a fine piece of water, and throughout a scene of elegance and refinement'. So it remains over 200 years later.

gambled away the family wealth in the late 19th century, disposed of many of the contents, including superb portraits by Gainsborough, and finally was forced to sell the estate in 1901.

The purchaser was Frederick Cawley MP (later became 1st Lord Cawley), a wealthy Lancashire cotton finisher who brought a new lease of life to Berrington. He redecorated the house around

(Above) A posthumous portrait of Thomas Harley, the builder of the house; after Henry Edridge (Library)

(Left) The entrance front

(Right) Rodney's battleship, the 'Sandwich', being attacked by the French at the Battle of Martinique in 1780. Detail from one of a group of battle paintings in the Dining Room celebrating Rodney's victories. His son married Thomas Harley's daughter, and their descendants inherited Berrington

TOUR OF THE HOUSE

THE MARBLE HALL

This room is typical of the formal entrance halls in 18th-century country houses, where important visitors would be received. The family would normally have used the back door, which was originally in Lady Cawley's Room.

CEILING AND FLOOR

The ceiling appears to be domed, but in fact the central section is a flat circle, carried on low arches and corner spandrels. It is echoed in the circular pattern of the floor, which is beautifully cut from black, white and green-grey marbles.

DECORATION

The style of the decoration was inspired by the severe French Neo-classicism which Holland introduced to England in the 1770s. Particularly French are the plaster roundels over the six corner doors, which are set within panels embellished with rosettes at the corners. The roundels are draped with swags of husks and contain trophies of arms in low relief – a reminder of more unsettled times,

when such entrance halls were used as armouries. Each of the trophies is slightly different, like much of Holland's seemingly repetitive ornament in the house.

For this semi-public room Holland chose the robust Doric order, which can be distinguished by the block-like mutules in the cornice and the triglyphs in the frieze immediately below.

The room was painted the present colours by Lord Cawley around 1908 – buff and gold on the ceiling, grey-green on the walls. It was probably first painted in plainer stone and white shades, to match the architectural character of the room.

DOORS

The doors are veneered in Spanish mahogany and are outstanding examples of 18th-century craftsmanship. The gilt locks and handles are probably also 18th-century, but must have been added later, as they are too large for the doors.

The door facing the entrance is emphasised with a pedimented doorcase (which includes a honeysuckle frieze), because it opens into the Staircase Hall and originally provided a vista right through the centre of the house to the back door. The four flanking doors were included mainly for the sake of symmetry: two open into cupboards, and two are false.

(Right) One of the Neo-classical plaster roundels of trophies of arms in the Marble Hall. Each is slightly different

(Left) The Marble Hall

TAPESTRIES

The fixed frames, which feature the *guttae* ('tear-drops') of the Doric order, were designed to hold paintings, but these were sold by the 7th Lord Rodney in the late 19th century. To replace them, around 1901 the 1st Lord Cawley commissioned tapestries from the Aubusson-Felletin factory based on paintings by the French artist Nicolas Lancret (1690–1743).

ON LEFT WALL:

Detail from *Le Feu*, from a set of four paintings depicting the four elements.

ON RIGHT WALL:

Le Jeu de Colin-Maillard au Jardin
(*Blind Man's Buff*)
The original painting was formerly in the Sans Souci palace, Potsdam, but was destroyed during the Second World War.

FURNITURE

The postbox once stood in the Staircase Hall, where it would be emptied by the butler. The postal rates are *engraved* on the letter scales – a mark of less inflationary times.

A set of six George IV hunting chairs.

The doorway on the right leads into the Library.

THE LIBRARY

Thomas Harley's great-grandfather, Robert, 1st Earl of Oxford, had assembled the finest private library in Britain, which was sold in 1744. His grandfather, the 2nd Earl, was a friend of Alexander Pope and Jonathan Swift. It was natural, therefore, that one of the principal rooms at Berrington should be a library. Alas, Harley's books were sold by the 7th Lord Rodney, who turned this into a billiard-room.

The 1st Lord Cawley removed the billiard-table and filled the shelves with books bought from Heaton Hall, Manchester. He also had the walls painted the present shades of duck-egg blue, pink and beige. In his day, guests assembled here before dinner; the room was also used for dances, when the carpet would be rolled back.

The Library

BOOKCASES

The fitted bookcases were designed for Harley by Holland to resemble classical façades, with shallow pediments and delicate Ionic pilasters, united by a frieze of square 'Greek key' pattern threaded with mistletoe berries.

DECORATION

OVER CHIMNEYPIECE:

The rectangular panel is attributed to Biagio Rebecca and depicts *Putti sacrificing to the blind Homer* (a common figure in libraries).

OVER DOORS:

The circular grisaille panels draped with garlands are of unidentified classical figures.

IN FRIEZE:

The rectangular panels are painted with allegories of the arts and a sacrifice.

CEILING

The portrait medallions, attributed to Rebecca, are painted to imitate high-relief stucco sculpture. As one would expect in a library, they represent English men of letters. From the fireplace, reading clockwise, they are: Matthew Prior (poet, but also political ally of Robert Harley, 1st Earl of Oxford), John Milton, Alexander Pope, William Shakespeare, Geoffrey Chaucer, Isaac Newton, Francis Bacon and Joseph Addison.

The central section is very similar to that Holland had recently designed for Lord Clive's Dressing Room at Claremont.

In order to protect the fragile ceiling from footfalls in the bedroom above, Sir Hubert Worthington raised the floor of the latter slightly. The ceiling has also had to survive a serious flood in recent years.

FIREPLACE

The steel grate and fireplace incorporate a fireback cast with Thomas Harley's arms.

FURNITURE

The pier-glasses with roundels, the console tables between the windows, and the curtain boxes with honeysuckle cresting are all original.

The Kirckman harpsichord, lent by Dr Richard Bulmer, was once part of the outstanding furniture collection formed by Harold Charles Moffatt at Goodrich Court.

CARPET

The beautiful Axminster carpet, in tones of carmine pink, cobalt blue and buff, was probably woven *c.*1825–50. Corrosive chemicals in the blue dye have caused these areas to wear particularly badly. Vital conservation work took place on this carpet during 2003.

CHANDELIER

The finely carved and gilded 18th-century chandelier was bought by the 1st Lord Cawley, who had it converted to electricity.

THE DINING ROOM

This is the largest room in the house, in which Harley celebrated the brilliant marriages made by his daughters Anne and Martha. It has a higher ceiling than elsewhere, which allowed him to hang the full-length portraits of Admiral Rodney and George and Martha Drummond he commissioned from Gainsborough. Sadly, these were sold in the 1880s, but the battle pictures commemorating Rodney's greatest triumphs survive.

Harley had begun his career as a wine merchant, and doubtless kept a good cellar at Berrington. Although the kitchen was in the basement immediately below, servants had to bring food to table by a circuitous route using the back stairs on the opposite side of the building.

The 1st Lord Cawley installed a dumb waiter and a screen (since removed), behind which the food would be served. In his time, dinner was a formal affair, taken at 7.30, for which men changed into dinner jacket and stiff shirt. Meals were substantial, consisting of soup, fish, main course, sweet and dessert.

DECORATION

When Lord Torrington visited in 1784, the walls were apparently painted 'flesh coloured'. They were painted the present shade of sage green around 1908 by the 1st Lord Cawley. Lady Cawley had the doorcases painted white; they had previously been picked out in gold.

The central roundel in the Dining Room ceiling depicts the Feast of the Gods – appropriate for such a room

CEILING

Appropriately for a dining-room, the central inset roundel was painted in the style of Biagio Rebecca with a composite scene based on Raphael's *Banquet of the Gods* and *The Council* in the Villa Farnesina, Rome. The appropriate classical deities, Bacchus, god of wine, and Ceres, goddess of corn, appear in the two rectangular panels.

FIREPLACE

The marble chimneypiece is the finest in the house and was a gift to Harley from Bell Lloyd, a friend since his schooldays at Westminster, whom he had rescued from financial ruin. It was installed between 1801 and 1804. The decoration seems to refer to Admiral Rodney's naval triumphs.

The upright panels show (on the left) a man carrying a crane (symbolising vigilance), with a battleship in full sail and a naval fort at his feet; and (on the right) a figure of Britannia holding a 'Cap of Liberty' and an olive branch with a cornucopia (symbolising freedom, peace and plenty), and with Britannia's shield and trident at her feet. The rods on which the figures stand are wreathed with vine leaves – perhaps an allusion to Harley's years in the wine trade.

The original central plaque was silver and depicted in low relief *The Sacrifice of Iphigenia*, which made possible the greatest naval expedition in classical mythology, of the Greek ships to Troy. Alas, it was sold by the 7th Lord Rodney. The 1st Lord Cawley inserted the marble replacement and the magnificent 18th-century steel grate. The brackets which supported the Edwardian glass smoke hood still survive.

PICTURES

The four large battle pictures depict episodes in the War of American Independence, in which Admiral Rodney played a prominent role by defeating the French and Spanish fleets supporting the rebellious American colonists.

ON WALL RIGHT OF WINDOWS:

THOMAS LUNY (1759–1837)
The Battle of the Saints, 1782
Signed and dated 1785
It records the second episode in the battle between Dominica and Guadeloupe on 12 April 1782 – the surrender at sunset of the French flagship, the *Ville de Paris* (a present to Louis XVI from the citizens of Paris). The victory did much to restore British prestige in the War of American Independence and earned Rodney his peerage.

LEFT OF FIREPLACE:

THOMAS LUNY (1759–1837)
The Battle of Martinique, 1780
Signed and dated 1786
Rodney's flagship *Sandwich* is being attacked by three French ships at once in the Battle of Martinique on 17 April 1780. The French Admiral was subsequently obliged to retreat in what turned out to be a pyrrhic victory for the British. But the episode reflected great credit on Rodney, who managed to extricate himself from an awkward situation brought about by the gross blunder of his leading captain, who had disregarded orders.

OVER FIREPLACE:

?After HENRY EDRIDGE (1769–1821)
Thomas Harley, MP (1730–1804)
A posthumous portrait of the builder of Berrington.

RIGHT OF FIREPLACE:

After RICHARD PATON (1717–91)
The Moonlight Battle, 1780
It depicts the blowing-up of the Spanish 70-gun

The Battle of the Saints by Thomas Luny, in the Dining Room

ship, *Santo Domingo*, off Cape St Vincent during the action of 16 January 1780, known as the Moonlight Battle, when Rodney was on his way to relieve the siege of Gibraltar. The larger, original version is in the National Maritime Museum.

OVER LARGE SIDEBOARD:

THOMAS LUNY (1759–1837)
The Battle of the Saints, 1782
Signed and dated 1785
It records the famous manoeuvre which Rodney was the first British seaman to employ, at the Battle of the Saints on 12 April 1782. In the *Formidable* he broke through the centre of the French line followed by his division, which closed in and raked the enemy's vessels with its broadsides. Then, the wind fortunately changing, Rodney was able to repeat the attack in the reverse direction.

FURNITURE

The dining-table is Victorian. The footstool was used by Elizabeth, Lady Cawley, as she was a short woman.

The dining-chairs were probably made in Portugal or in Portuguese Goa. The remainder came from the sale of Heaton Hall, Manchester, in 1902.

The Grecian sideboard, mahogany, *c.*1800–5 was formerly at Finborough Hall, Suffolk, lent by Charles Pettiward.

The large and two lesser side-tables veneered in mahogany and satinwood were bought with the house by the 1st Lord Cawley.

FLANKING LARGE SIDE-TABLE:

A plate-warmer in the form of an urn, by Gillow of Lancaster.

A matching cellaret. Hot water was stored in the urn, which the butler would use for washing glasses in the zinc-lined drawer below, which pulled out to form a sink. The bottom drawer held six decanters.

CERAMICS

ON DINING-TABLE:

Dresden service hand-painted with flowers, *c.*1840.

ON SIDE-TABLE:

Chinese Export porcelain slop pail, *c.*1780, from a bedroom set.

The Chinese Export punchbowl, which celebrates Admiral Rodney's victory at the Battle of the Saints in 1782, was given to Berrington by the late Lord Croft.

The doorway on the fireplace side of the Dining Room leads to the Staircase Hall.

THE STAIRCASE HALL

The Staircase Hall fills the middle of the house and shows Holland's mastery of complex and dramatic spatial effects. One enters immediately beneath a massive coffered arch on axis with a vista through the centre of the house from the front door to Lady Cawley's Room. As one turns out of the shadow into the light, the full height of the central top-lit space suddenly reveals itself. This picturesque effect owes much to the fantasy views of the Italian designer Piranesi.

The room was painted its present colours by the 1st Lord Cawley *c.*1908.

STAIRCASE

The staircase rises gently round three sides of the room, with a bronzed cast-iron balustrade of lyres and an elegant mahogany handrail. The balustrade continues along the landing on the fourth side, which is supported by the coffered arch. Within the main arch is another smaller arch, centred on a door providing access to the back stairs, which were used mainly by the servants and so, unlike the main stairs, connect with the attic floor and the basement.

The columns in the Staircase Hall are made of ochre- and grey-veined scagliola in imitation of Siena marble

The Staircase Hall

The full subtlety of Holland's composition is best appreciated from under the domed skylight.

SKYLIGHT

This is constructed of delicate metal ribs that meet in rosettes, with further circular ribs centred on these intersections.

CEILING

The plasterwork compartments framing the skylight are painted white with grisaille medallions against a pink ground. The original decoration was probably rather plainer.

FLOOR

The floor is made from contrasting slabs of York stone and slate.

SCULPTURE

LEFT OF ARCH:

E. G. PAPWORTH the Younger (b. 1832)
James Bancroft (c. 1798–1888), 1869
The late Lady Cawley's maternal grandfather was a colliery worker who rose to be a railway director and philanthropist.

RIGHT OF ARCH:

ODOARDO FANTACCHIOTTI
Hannah Lee, née Dracup (1816–94), 1877
The late Lady Cawley's grandmother. The bust was sculpted in Florence and eventually reached England despite being dropped in the harbour at Marseilles.

TAPESTRIES

The fixed frames, like those in the Marble Hall, were designed to contain naval scenes, which were sold by the 7th Lord Rodney. The 1st Lord Cawley replaced them with two further Aubusson-Felletin tapestries after Nicolas Lancret (1690–1743).

UNDER STAIRS:

A Concert

OVER STAIRS:

Mlle Camargo dancing
Maria de Camargo (1710–70) was one of the originators of modern ballet.

LADY CAWLEY'S ROOM

In 1887 it was called the Sportsmen's Room, and so may have been decorated with sporting prints and used to store riding gear. The left-hand window contained the back door until the bathroom tower was built on to the adjoining room in the 1890s.

Towards the end of her long life, Vivienne, Lady Cawley used this as a comfortable sitting-room, where she enjoyed watching television. Following her death in 1978, the room has been arranged to commemorate the Cawley family and reflect their life at Berrington since 1901.

DECORATION

The room was covered in dark brown wallpaper until the 1970s, when the Trust hung the present wallpaper, which is based on an 18th-century pattern found at Clandon Park in Surrey.

FIREPLACE

The cast-iron grate and decorative steel surround were inserted by the 2nd Lord Cawley when he inherited Berrington in 1937. This replaces a Victorian green-tiled fireplace.

PICTURES

ON WINDOW WALL:

Some of Lady Cawley's photographs, including those of herself and her mother-in-law, the 1st Lady Cawley, when she presented her daughter-in-law at Court in 1914. A wedding group at Broughton Park, Salford, in 1912 is below. Above is Thomas Cawley (1806–75), father of the 1st Lord Cawley.

RIGHT OF CHIMNEYPIECE:

A lithograph of Berrington from the south in the early 19th century, showing the bronze cannon captured by Admiral Rodney at the 'Moonlight Battle' in 1780. They were transferred to nearby Brampton Bryan later in the century.

The other family portraits and miniatures are of the Lee family, ancestors of Vivienne, Lady Cawley, who were also in the Lancashire cotton industry.

The silhouettes are mostly of the 3rd Lord Cawley and his brothers at Eton in the late 1920s and '30s.

Lady Cawley's Room

FURNITURE

The satinwood bureau and the compartmented centre-table were bequeathed by Dame Joan Evans.

The north Italian commode was left to the Trust by Dame Joan Evans.

SCULPTURE

ON MANTELPIECE:

A bronze statuette of a parakeet holding a feather from Lady Cawley's parrot.

THE BACK HALL

In 1887 this was called the Justice Room, and so perhaps was used as the estate office. When the bathroom tower was added to the courtyard façade outside in the 1890s, a new door opening into it was created. The room then became the Back Hall, which the family used as the day-to-day entrance to the house. The tower was demolished in the 1960s, but the door was retained as the rear entrance.

FIREPLACE

The chimneypiece was removed some time after 1937 to a courtyard room but has been reinstated by the National Trust.

DECORATION

The ceiling was redecorated and the central rosette gilded in the 1970s.

FURNITURE

FLANKING BACK DOOR:

The mahogany cabinets were originally one piece and were used for storing coats.

On the hatstand are the 'Anthony Eden' hat used by the 3rd Lord Cawley when at the Bar, and his mother's Red Cross and gardening hats.

The walking sticks include a 'saw' stick and a prototype of the modern shooting-stick.

The seahorses are fittings from a Venetian gondola.

PICTURES

LEFT OF FIREPLACE:

GIACOMO GUARDI (1764–1835)
View of Venice
Gouache

RIGHT OF FIREPLACE:

GIACOMO GUARDI (1764–1835)
View of Venice
Gouache

Cartoon of the 20th Hussars, Stephen Cawley's regiment by Snaffles. He was killed at Nery during the retreat from Mons in 1914. A letter of condolence from Winston Churchill to his brother Harold Cawley MP hangs nearby.

EDMUND DULAC (1882–1953)
Cartoon of Winston Churchill as 'The Pirate King', 1921

GODFREY HAYMAN
Capt. John Cawley (1919–43)
A posthumous portrait of the 3rd Lord Cawley's youngest brother, who was killed in action near Tunis in 1943.

THE BUSINESS ROOM

In the 1880s this was called the Smoking Room, and it was probably always a male preserve. Alterations seem to have been made soon after the room was first conceived and again in more recent times: there was originally a false door on the right of the fireplace.

CEILING

The square ceiling contains four painted lozenges of female figures representing the Four Seasons in the style of Rebecca. The artist had already painted a similar set at Harewood House near Leeds.

DECORATION

The decoration here is less ambitious than in the other principal rooms on the ground floor. Decades of tobacco smoke had blackened the ceiling, and

so in 1975 it was decided to redecorate following evidence of the original colours discovered after careful investigation.

FIREPLACE

A contemporary fire grate from one of the bedrooms has been substituted within the original marble chimneypiece for the unsuitable late Victorian one.

PICTURES

OVER FIREPLACE:

Sir WILLIAM LLEWELLYN, PRA (1858–1941)
Frederick, 1st Lord Cawley, PC (1850–1937)
Dated 1920
Painted in his Cabinet Minister's uniform. Not a good likeness, according to the 3rd Lord Cawley.

ON WALL LEFT OF DOOR:

MAURICE CODNER (1888–1958)
Robert, 2nd Lord Cawley (1877–1954)
Painted in 1953.

ON WALL RIGHT OF DOOR:

MICHAEL WOODS
Frederick, 3rd Lord Cawley (b. 1913)
In 1954 he inherited Berrington, which he surrendered to the Treasury three years later in part-payment of death duties.

A photograph shows the 7th Lord Rodney returning to Berrington from his honeymoon in 1891. He was the last Rodney owner of Berrington, selling the estate to the 3rd Lord Cawley's grandfather in 1901.

FURNITURE

The tall bookcase contains finely bound books, the remnant of the library from Finborough Hall, Suffolk salvaged when the house was given up by the Pettiward family in 1935. Given to Berrington in 2002 by Charles Pettiward.

The original pier-glass returned here from the Boudoir in 1975.

The handsome mahogany writing-desk is in the Chippendale style.

CERAMICS

A large Copeland imitation-Chinese garden stool under the Chinese Chippendale table.

The Business Room

The Boudoir

THE BOUDOIR

This room has always been used by the women of the house. Double doors on both sides protected their privacy, and servants could bring refreshments from the kitchen below via the door to the right of the alcove, which connected with the back stairs. The cupboard behind the shutters was designed to hold two chamberpots.

During the Second World War the room became Lady Cawley's office, when she was commandant of the hospital at Berrington. The ink stain on the floor was caused in the 1930s by a burglar who upset a silver inkwell.

CEILING

The barrel ceiling is very simply decorated with bands of blue and pink, framing an oval of Venus on a cloud playing with cupids. The frieze alternates rosettes with an unidentified species of flightless bird.

ALCOVE

Curved alcoves often appear at the end of important 18th-century rooms, such as the Dining Room at Kedleston and the Library at Kenwood. But here Holland has created an unusual spatial effect by introducing a shallow and wide alcove that fills almost the entire *long* side of the Boudoir. It is topped by a fan-shaped semi-dome behind a screen of blue Ionic columns and pilasters which supports an entablature of differing swags of flowers. The columns are made from scagliola, a mixture of pulverised gypsum, sand and, in this case, lapis lazuli (to create the blue colour), which was polished to resemble marble. The technique was perfected in the mid-18th century.

DECORATION

The thin gilt wall-frames are an early Victorian addition. The white lattice-work lincrusta wallpaper was probably put up by the 6th Lord Rodney after his marriage in 1850.

FIREPLACE

The original fireplace was sold by the 7th Lord Rodney, who put in the present late Victorian model as a poor substitute.

CURTAINS

The curtain box is probably contemporary with the room.

FURNITURE

An early Louis XV commode with a *brocatelle* (variegated) marble top.

The high quality mid-18th-century giltwood armchairs, with lion's-mask crests to the back and lion's-head

A capital and lapis lazuli scagliola pilaster in the Boudoir

finials to the arms, are probably from a set formerly at the Cope family house at Bramshill, Hampshire.

ON COMMODE:

A fine French clock by Mignolet with a gilt bronze cage on a marble base. It once belonged to the Comte de Flahaut and reputedly to Marie Antoinette.

FLANKING COMMODE:

A pair of gilt Venetian mirrors, with glasses engraved with dancing figures with birds.

ON CHIMNEYPIECE:

A French clock, c.1785, flanked by a pair of white marble and gilt bronze vases.

The giltwood embroidered fire-screen also belonged to the Comte de Flahaut.

AGAINST WINDOW WALL:

A 19th-century guéridon (small table), mounted with a Louis XV blue Sèvres plate.

PICTURES

OVER COMMODE:

Ascribed to JAN VAN GOYEN (1596–1656)
A Coastal Scene
Dated 1640
Panel

LEFT OF CHIMNEYPIECE:

A group of 18th-century French engravings after Jean-Michel Moreau the Younger (1741–1814).

ABOVE CHIMNEYPIECE:

The miniatures include two of Jane Digby (1807–81), one of the great Regency beauties. At seventeen she married Lord Ellenborough, but was soon being pursued by Prince Felix Schwartzenberg, by whom she had a child. A spectacularly messy divorce in 1830 obliged her to live abroad, where she captivated King Ludwig I of Bavaria and the French novelist Balzac, who called her 'this peaches and cream woman, so delicate, so gentle, with such a tender face crowned with shining fawn-coloured hair'. In later life she travelled in the Middle East, marrying Sheikh Medjuel el Mezrab.

The five silk pictures were embroidered by the 1st Lady Cawley.

FANS

Two framed French fans. The one painted with a classical scene depicts *Coriolanus begged not to attack Rome by his family*. It belonged to Queen Hortense of Holland, the Comte de Flahaut's mistress. She was the daughter of Joséphine de la Pagerie, who later became Napoleon's first wife; she herself married Napoleon's brother Louis, King of Holland.

THE DRAWING ROOM

This was Thomas Harley's principal sitting-room, balancing the Library on the opposite side of the Marble Hall and with good views of the park from the large windows. In 1796 Lady Sykes of Sledmere in Yorkshire thought it 'very elegantly finished and furnished'. During the Second World War it became a sitting-room for the nurses working in the convalescent hospital in the servants' block.

It still retains its original white and gold curtain boxes and broad pier-glasses with sprays of leaves and garlands above. The panelling is a later addition.

DECORATION

Lady Sykes considered 'the room and furniture deserved better hangings, being only papered with a four-penny paper, or some paltry stuff'. In 1900 the walls were covered with a Victorian green paper ornamented with white parrots. The 1st Lord Cawley had the walls painted white about 1908.

FIREPLACE

The chimneypiece was carved from white Carrara marble and is very similar to that Holland had designed for the Great Room at Claremont. The frieze of griffins contains a central plaque of Apollo

The Carrara marble chimneypiece in the Drawing Room contains a late 18th-century steel grate decorated with blue Wedgwood cameos

and a nymph before a Greek temple and pyramid, perhaps an allusion to Harley's interest in architecture. It is flanked by draped caryatids, again subtly differentiated.

The magnificent late 18th-century steel grate was bought by Lord Cawley around 1908 to replace the missing original. Very unusually, the front is decorated with Wedgwood blue jasper cameos. Before the fire was lit, the front would be removed to prevent the cameos cracking.

CEILING

This is the finest ceiling at Berrington and one of the most elaborate ever designed by Holland. In contrast to the French Neo-classicism of the Entrance Hall, it recalls the more delicate style of Robert Adam.

The central medallion depicts *Jupiter, Cupid and Venus*. The four smaller medallions feature other classical scenes: *The Arming of Aeneas* (over fireplace), *Hercules serving Queen Omphale* (over windows), *Venus and Adonis* (over door to Marble Hall) and *A Nymph crowning Cupid* (over door to Boudoir).

The medallions were painted in the style of Biagio Rebecca (1735–1808), ARA, who became one of the most successful decorative artists of the period, working for Adam at Kedleston and Harewood, and again for Holland at the Brighton Pavilion.

The decorative plasterwork may be by William Pearce, who had worked for Holland at Claremont. Within the central circular border of wave-like Vitruvian scroll pattern, four putti harness seahorses with blue ribbons. The rectangular panels either side contain alternate medallions of boys and white stucco plaster fans within a guilloche border.

FURNITURE

In 1796 this room was furnished with 'chairs in Chenille composed of bunches of Flowers, all different, [taken] from Mrs Wright's patterns by the Miss Harleys extremely fine. The housekeeper lamented they could not prevent gentlemen sitting down on the chairs, tho' there are a second set for use. There are only eight of the worked chairs completed.' Sadly, these have all gone.

The room is now furnished with French furniture and works of art from the Elmar Digby collection which complement Holland's French-inspired

The Drawing Room

decoration. The Hon. A.E. Digby inherited some pieces from his mother, wife of the 10th Lord Digby, and collected others. The collection was given to the Trust by Mrs C.V. Lawson in 1981.

The three commodes with kingwood and tulip-wood parquetry and gilt bronze mounts are of the *Régence* or early Louis XV period (*c*.1710–*c*.1730). The two flanking the chimneypiece have *griotte* marble tops. The one on the right is signed by the *ébéniste* M. Criard and belonged, together with several other objects in the collection, to the Comte de Flahaut (1785–1870), natural son of the politician Talleyrand. Flahaut was a general and ADC to the Emperor Napoleon and eventually ambassador in London for Napoleon III. In 1817 he married the Hon. Margaret Mercer Elphinstone, and through their eldest daughter Emily the collection passed to the Digby family until it was sold in 1951, when some pieces were rescued by Mr Digby.

AT END OF ROOM:

A Régence (1715–23) Boulle writing desk, known as a *bureau Mazarin*.

A small 18th-century kidney table (table à rognon) in the manner of Pierre Roussel (1723–82) with a floral marquetry top and sliding front in the form of book spines.

The giltwood furniture is mainly English in the French taste, but the smallest piece is part of a Louis XVI giltwood *lit à la duchesse* (a *chaise-longue* in two parts).

The piano with gilt bronze mounts is an Erard of *c*.1914.

OBJETS D'ART

ON MANTELPIECE:

A Louis XV white marble clock by Julien Leroy, and a pair of cassolettes (urn candlesticks) which belonged to Flahaut.

Busts of the French philosophers Rousseau and Voltaire.

IN SHOWCASE:

A collection of enamel, ivory, tortoiseshell, silver and niello (Russian black enamel and silver) snuff boxes and sewing boxes, seals, watches and other small *objets d'art*.

ON BOULLE WRITING DESK:

The Comte de Flahaut's pen tray.

CERAMICS

Chinese celadon vases.

A fine pair of Imari ice-pails with gilt bronze ring handles.

PICTURES

After ALLAN RAMSAY (1713–84)
Jean-Jacques Rousseau (1712–78)
Philosopher and one of the central figures of the French Enlightenment.

The engravings include portraits of:
The engraver Jean-Baptiste Massé (1687–1767)
The painter Charles Lebrun (1619–90)
The Marquis de Marigny (1727–81), brother of Mme de Pompadour and superintendent of the King's buildings.

THE FIRST-FLOOR LANDING

This has communicating galleries on three sides, which are subtly unified by screens of paired columns and pilasters. The shafts are made from ochre and grey-veined scagliola to resemble Siena marble. The Corinthian capitals are plaster (repaired in 1861 and 1891), the bases grey marble. They support a frieze, featuring dolphins with entwined tails, which runs around the fourth side of the landing and possibly refers to the marriage of Harley's daughter to Admiral Rodney's son.

The decoration of the overdoors is a simpler version of that in the Marble Hall.

SCULPTURE

IN LEFT-HAND NICHE:

A 19th-century Italian figure of a girl in alabaster and marble.

IN RIGHT-HAND NICHE:

A marble group of Hercules bringing back Alcestis on Charon's ferry, with a relief of *Hercules being rowed to the rescue of Hesione*. Italian, *c*.1800.

The Nursery

THE NURSERY

The Nursery, with its axial view of Holland's courtyard, is shown with furnishings, pictures and toys from before the First World War.

TOYS

Among the few remaining family toys is a magic wand from a primitive conjuring set owned by Lord Cawley's great-uncle, James Bancroft. The rest, including the miniature four-poster and its inmate, are from the collections of Mrs Sandford and several other local people, who have generously augmented the contents of the room.

The enormous rocking horse, formerly at Bockleton Court in Worcestershire, was given by Miss Prescott; it has panniers for additional riders at each end.

PICTURES

ABOVE ROCKING HORSE:

Two coloured nursery prints by John Hassall (1868–1948). His work was a favourite for the nursery with artistic parents before the First World War.

OVER MANTELPIECE:

*A nursery frieze, c.*1905, by Cecil Aldin (1870–1935).

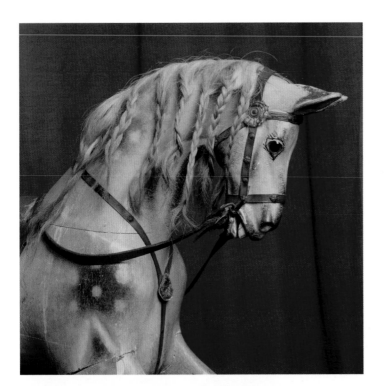

(Left) The rocking horse in the Nursery

(Below) The 1st Lord Cawley with his four sons in front of Berrington in 1908. Three were to die in the First World War

Hunting clothes and uniforms in the White Dressing Room

CARPET

The hand-knotted carpet is from a design of *c.*1897 by the Arts and Crafts architect C.F.A. Voysey and was made by Morton & Co. in Donegal. This pattern of stylised flowering and evergreen trees with swans and deer was also used for wallpaper, friezes and upholstery fabric. Until recently the carpet was at nearby Eye Manor, home of the late Mr Christopher Sandford, whose father bought it new for his home in Ireland.

THE WHITE DRESSING ROOM

CLOTHES

The hunting clothes and uniforms belonged to members of the Cawley family, especially Major Stephen Cawley, 20th Hussars, who was killed in action at Nery in September 1914.

THE OVAL ROOM

The display in this room is dedicated to three of Sir Frederick and Lady Cawley's sons who were killed in the First World War. The sombre atmosphere has been created to convey how Lady Cawley might have felt as she sat by the fire and reminisced about her sons. There are letters and tributes which visitors are encouraged to look at. There is also a display of some of the men's uniforms and their other military items.

THE CORNER DRESSING ROOM AND BEDROOM

These rooms depict the homecoming in May 1891 of the 7th Lord Rodney with his new wife Corisande from their honeymoon. The Dressing Room includes an 1840 marble-topped washstand complete with bedroom china.

In the bedroom are examples of the sorts of items which might have been used by her Ladyship, including perfumes and creams placed on the dressing table, which visitors are invited to examine and touch. A replica wedding dress, copied from a detailed description and a photograph, which can be seen in the bedroom, is also on display.

THE BACK STAIRS AND THE SERVANTS' QUARTERS

The servants' quarters are divided between the attics and the basement, and the three ranges of two-storey buildings which form the courtyard at the back of the house. The restaurant is in what was once the Servants' Hall, the shop in the old Harness Room, and the tea-room in the old Kitchen. It is hoped to open up more of these rooms to visitors. At present the Trust shows the Laundry (in the left-hand block) and the Dairy (at the far end of the right-hand block).

The Stable Block

The Laundry

THE LAUNDRY

The Laundry, with its adjacent Drying Room, was originally in the north end of the east service block. It seems to have been moved to its present position, in what had been a secondary kitchen, in the late 19th century. Most of the machinery shown here dates from that period.

Clothes would be washed in the tubs at the ends of the room, wrung out through the large mangle, and then hung to dry on the broad rails of the cast-iron drying frames. These would be slid back gently into the large brick chamber, which was heated by pipes and by the central stove, which was also used to heat irons. When the clothes were dry, the frames would be slid out again, and garments removed for ironing. This system allowed clothes to be dried quickly and

in bad weather, but Stevenson's *House Architecture* (1880) thought it cumbersome and inferior to traditional methods: 'Even with the most perfect ventilation, they can never, if dried in darkness, have the purity and freshness which is given by the sun and open air of a bleaching green'. Berrington's original drying ground still survives next to the Walled Garden.

The Dairy

THE DAIRY

Herefordshire is famous for the breed of white-faced beef cattle which originated in the county, but it has also always produced good dairy stock. Before the era of mechanical refrigeration and rapid transport, it was important that estates such as Berrington should be able to make their own cream, butter and cheese. That was done in this cool room.

The deceptively simple decoration was designed by Henry Holland and has survived almost unchanged since the 1780s. As such, it is among the first and the finest examples of the Louis XVI style in Britain. The plain, tiled walls are divided into alternating broad and narrow compartments by thin green bands of Neo-classical 'Greek key' pattern. The round-headed niches, in which bowls of cream would be left to separate, flank and echo the doorway in the semicircular apse at the far end, which led into the Larder. The stone and pitch floor is a slightly simpler version of that in the Marble Hall.

THE GARDEN AND PARK

HISTORY

Berrington lies in one of the most beautiful parts of north Herefordshire, between Leominster and Ludlow, with grand views to the west and north across a broad valley, through which flows a tributary of the River Lugg. The panorama comprises, from left to right, Westhope Hill and Burton Hill eleven miles away; the long northern ridge of the Black Mountains 20–25 miles away; the Brecon Beacons 39 miles away, and the hills beyond Kington and Eywood; then Radnor Forest about 20 miles away. Further to the right Eye church is a prominent landmark. Still further to the north-west and about four miles away the impressive Iron Age hill-fort of Croft Ambrey (also the property of the National Trust) is visible on the skyline.

Thomas Harley seems to have begun work on laying out the park at Berrington even before his new house was erected. In August 1775, around the time he bought the estate, Harley was staying at nearby Eywood, when he encountered 'Capability'

Brown, who was remodelling the park there for Harley's brother, the 4th Earl of Oxford (both house and park have since disappeared). Brown rode over to Berrington and seems to have suggested improvements to the park and the best site for a new house. However, there is no record of another visit until 1780, the same year that he sent his foreman, John Spyers, to make a survey plan of the estate. Brown was paid £400 in July 1781 and received a further £1,200 over the next fourteen months. In his usual fashion, he created an open sweep of grassy parkland from the steps of the west front, over a ha-ha (which has recently been restored), and down to the Pool, an eye-catching fourteen-acre lake, in which he built a four-acre wooded island. This later became a favourite spot for the Cawley grandchildren, where they would fish and mess about in boats. The National Trust has laid out a circuit walk around Brown's park and lake, from which you can enjoy views back to the

The park from the Pool

TOUR OF THE GARDEN

house framed by artfully positioned clumps of oak, lime, beech and ash.

From the 1840s the Rodneys gradually built a formal flower garden around the house. More radical changes were made in the Edwardian era, when the 1st Lord Cawley commissioned Dobies of Chester to create a garden between the house and the triumphal arch. At its height, it comprised no fewer than 36 beds filled with garish zinnias and asters. This was extremely labour-intensive to maintain, and since the Second World War has had to be drastically simplified. In 1906 Lord Cawley expanded the Victorian shrubbery to the north of the house to provide a very necessary shelter belt for the garden.

The National Trust maintains the 11.5 acres of garden and 439 acres of park and woodland, which are on heavy, neutral soil, with a staff of two gardeners, who have replanted the Walled Garden (see p. 33) and filled the borders with a wide range of shrubs and flowers to provide colour and interest throughout the visitor season.

THE ENTRANCE DRIVE

All that is left of the 1st Lord Cawley's Edwardian garden south of the Walled Garden are the fountain and the avenue of golden yews, clipped into balls, which flank the path running across the garden from the arch to the back of the house. The 3rd Lord Cawley planted many of the flowering trees and shrubs that line the curving carriage drive. They include Persian Lilac, Purple-leafed Hazel and double-flowered gorse.

THE WALLED GARDEN

This was originally the kitchen garden, but like many others fell out of use during the Second World War because of the high cost of upkeep.

The pergola on the south-facing exterior wall is draped with purple wisteria and flanked by beds planted with shrubs like Abutilon and *Buddleja colvilei* and climbers such as the rare Yellow-flowered Marrow (*Thladiantha oliveri*, male form).

Herefordshire is famous for its orchards, and the National Trust has replanted the central area of the Walled Garden with pre-20th-century varieties of apples which have fallen out of cultivation. The project has been supported by the National Council for the Conservation of Plants and Gardens, because these old varieties are not only of historical interest, but also a source of future plant-breeding material. Among the more evocative local names are 'Herefordshire Beefing', a small, dark crimson apple dating back to the 1700s, and 'Lady's Finger of Hereford East', a slender yellow cider apple first bred in 1884, which had become almost extinct.

Pears are trained as cordons against the north-east wall at the far end of the garden. Most of these varieties originated in France or Belgium, where many of the best dessert pears were first raised during the 19th century. They include the ancient 'Jargonelle' variety, which ripens in August, and 'Beurre Superfin', which was first raised in Angers in 1837 and is one of the best pears in cultivation. Plums such as 'Rivers' Early Prolific', morello cherries, figs, mulberries and quinces are also grown here.

THE WOODLAND GARDEN

Among the old woodland and the Victorian shrubberies to the north-east of the house is a large collection of azaleas and rhododendrons, some hybridised by the 3rd Lord Cawley. These are generally at their best in May. There are also Weeping Ash, the Handkerchief Tree and maples here.

(Left)
The garden from
the east

(Right)
The Walled
Garden

FAMILY TREE
OF THE RODNEYS

Owners of Berrington are shown
in CAPITALS

* denotes portrait in the house

Eagles do not bring forth doves

George Brydges Rodney* = (1) Jane Compton
Admiral Lord Rodney   (1730–57)
(1719–92)   m. 1753

THOMAS HARLEY, MP* (1730–1804) = Anne Bangham
5th son of 3rd Earl of Oxford   d. 1798
builder of Berrington   m. 1752

GEORGE, = ANNE	Martha	Sarah	Elizabeth	Margaret
2nd LORD (1758–	(1757–1788)	(1760–1837)	(1763–1824)	(1765–1830)
RODNEY 1840)	= George	= Robert Auriel	= David Murray	= Sir John
(1753– m. 1781	Drummond	9th Earl	m. 1788	Boyd Bt
1802)	(1758–89)	of Kinnoul		m. 1784
	m. 1799	m. 1781		

GEORGE, = Charlotte	THOMAS,	Rev. Spencer,	Robert = Anne
3rd LORD RODNEY* Morgan*	4th LORD	5th LORD	(1786–1826) Dennett
(1782–1842) (d. 1878)	RODNEY	RODNEY	
m. 1819	(1784–1843)	(1785–1846)	

ROBERT, 6th LORD RODNEY = Sarah Singleton* (d. 1882)
(1820–64)   m. 1850

GEORGE, = (1) Corisande Guest* (b. 1870)	Patience = Robert William Daker Harley
7th LORD RODNEY* m. 1891 div. 1902	Anne (1846–1907)
(1857–1909) = (2) Charlotte Probyn	(1854– of Brampton Bryan
sells Berrington in 1901 (d. 1939) m. 1903	1918) m. 1818

FAMILY TREE
OF THE CAWLEYS

I desire, I believe, I have

Lee Lee* = Anne Cocksey
(1782–1837)   (1791–1871)

Henry Lee* = Hannah   James Bancroft*   Thomas Cawley* = Harriet
(1817–1904)   Dracup*   (c.1798–1888)   (1806–75)   Bird
of Sedgeley Hall, Prestwich   (1816–94)   colliery worker   of Bunbury, Cheshire
cotton manufacturer   railway director   agent to Lord
MP for Southampton   philanthropist   Tollemache

Harold Lee (1851– = Agnes   FREDERICK CAWLEY* = Elizabeth
        1936)   Bancroft   cr. 1st BARON CAWLEY 1918   Smith*
of Broughton Park   (1850–1937)   (d. 1930)
Manchester   MP for Prestwich, Lancs. *buys*   m. 1876
                                          Berrington in 1901

Vivienne = ROBERT,   Capt. Harold   Maj. Stephen   Capt. Oswald   Hilda
Lee*   2nd LORD   Cawley, MP*   Cawley*   Cawley, MP*   Mary
(1877–1978) CAWLEY*   (1878–1915)   (1879–1914)   (1882–1918)
m. 1912   (1877–1954)   killed at Gallipoli   killed at Nery   killed at Merville

FREDERICK, = Rosemary Marsden   Stephen Cawley = Iris Marsden   Capt. John Cawley*
3rd LORD CAWLEY   (d. 2008)   (1915–95)   m. 1952   (1919–43)
(1913–2001)   m. 1944   killed in Tunisia

JOHN, 4th LORD CAWLEY   5 sons   1 daughter
        (b. 1946)

BERRINGTON AND ITS OWNERS

THOMAS HARLEY

As a younger son of the 3rd Earl of Oxford, Thomas Harley had to make his own way in the world. He began by marrying an heiress, Anne Bangham, in 1752. The same year he used her money and City connections to set up as a wine merchant in Aldersgate. The business flourished and diversified into supplying uniforms to the British Army, and in 1761 Harley became an alderman and MP for the City of London. As City sheriff in 1763, he was responsible for the public burning of the notorious issue no. 45 of John Wilkes's *North Britain* magazine, which had been condemned for 'seditious libel' against the King. Wilkes, however, was a popular figure in London; Horace Walpole described what happened next:

The mob rose; the greatest mob, says Mr Sheriff Blunt, that he has known in forty years. They were armed with that most bloody instrument, the mud out of the kennels; they hissed in the most murderous manner; broke Mr Sheriff Harley's coach-glass in the most frangent manner; scratched his forehead, so that he is forced to wear a little patch in the most becoming manner.

Harley's term as Lord Mayor in 1768 was marked by sadness and turmoil. His only son Edward died at the age of eleven, and he clashed again with Wilkes, who stood against him in the general election that year. Harley held on to his seat, but five days later Wilkes had his revenge when he was elected for the Middlesex constituency. Wilkes's supporters went on the rampage in the City, smashing every window in the Mansion House and parading a boot and petticoat from a gibbet (symbolising the deeply unpopular Prime Minister, Lord Bute, and his supposed mistress, Princess Augusta). Harley successfully quelled the riots, for which he received the thanks of Parliament. He was offered a pension, but cannily held out for 'something in the way of his profession'. In this fashion he managed to get the government contract to supply the clothing and wages of the army in North America. As the conflict with the rebellious American colonists intensified, so the contract grew: in 1777 alone he supplied over 40,000 pairs of mittens. In alliance with John Drummond, senior partner in the famous Charing Cross bank of that name, he remitted £17 million to pay the British forces between 1770 and 1783. It is estimated that Harley earned over £600,000 from these government contracts. The younger son had become a rich man, keen to retire from the hurly-burly of City politics and set himself up as a country gentleman.

He looked towards Herefordshire, where his family had lived at Brampton Bryan and Eywood for centuries. In 1774 he contested the Herefordshire seat which had previously been held by his elder brother, finally being elected in 1776. Around that date he bought the Berrington estate, which has spectacular views west towards the Black Mountains and the family estates in the Radnor forests. The rolling and well-wooded Herefordshire landscape was ideally suited for a great landscape park, and in the spring of 1778 Harley called in 'Capability' Brown to advise. (For details of his work, see p. 31.) Brown's name had probably been passed on by Harley's brother, the 4th Earl of Oxford, whose park at Eywood he had landscaped in 1775.

But Harley also wanted a house.

(Right) In 1768 Thomas Harley, as Lord Mayor, confronts the radical John Wilkes's rioting supporters, who have been parading a boot and petticoat from a gibbet (symbolising the hated Prime Minister, Lord Bute, and his supposed mistress, Princess Augusta). A grateful government awarded Harley a supply contract which helped to make his fortune

The Lodge, which was designed by Henry Holland in the form of a triumphal arch

BUILDING BERRINGTON

In his early years Brown had designed country houses at Croome Court and elsewhere, but when his landscape practice mushroomed, he turned over the architectural side of the business to his son-in-law, Henry Holland. If Harley needed any further recommendation, he could have asked John Drummond. For not only did both Brown and Holland bank at Drummonds, but in 1775–8 they had together built a smaller prototype of Berrington at Cadland in Hampshire for John Drummond's cousin Robert.

In 1778 Henry Holland was 33 and just beginning to be taken up by a small circle of Francophile Whig aristocrats. He made his name in 1776–8 designing their favourite London club, Brooks's in St James's, and went on to get the plum commission of his generation, remodelling Carlton House for the Prince of Wales. Holland was one of the pioneers in introducing the plainer French Neo-classical style, which from the 1770s gradually replaced Palladianism as the fashionable style for English country houses. But as he did not make his first visit to France until 1785, his understanding of the new taste seems to have been absorbed almost entirely from studying the illustrations in works like Jean François Neufforge's *Recueil élémentaire d'architecture* (1757–80), which sought to record 'the masculine, simple, and majestic manner of the ancient architects of Greece, and of the best modern architects'.

At Berrington the mood of Neo-classical severity is set at once by the lodge, which takes the form of a triumphal arch, perhaps as a reminder of Harley's career in the City, where triumphal arches marked the old Roman gateways into London until the

1760s. The windows are set directly into the smoothly cut stone without any form of mouldings. The only decorations are the cast-iron balustrade and the keystone over the central arch. Carefully judged proportion alone gives this building its presence.

From the lodge, the drive divides: day-to-day visitors would approach the house from the east, passing through another arch in the east service pavilion into a rectangular courtyard somewhat similar in feel to the forecourt of a Parisian town house. The north and south sides of the courtyard consist of two further service blocks, which also incorporate triumphal arches in the form of simple 'blind' recesses on their west façades and semi-circular, round-headed niches on their longer elevations. Yet more arches appear in the curving screens that link the pavilions to the house – one open to frame spectacular views of the Hereford-shire countryside.

The house itself is, if anything, even more severe – a rectangular box of two principal storeys, with a basement below and an attic floor and another balustrade above, which here runs round the entire building to disguise the pitched roof of Welsh slate. The carcase of the house and the service blocks were built from brick, cased in reddish-brown sandstone quarried a mile away at Shuttocks Hill and brought to the site along a specially constructed railway line.

The courtyard façade is relatively modest, the central three bays brought slightly forward and topped by a pediment. Just as at Cadland, the central three windows on the ground floor are set within round-headed recesses. Unusually, the principal, west, front faces the park and the best of the views. Set well forward from the flanking pavilions and towering above them, it dominates the landscape that slopes away to the south. Dominating the west front is the massive pedi-mented portico, which is supported by four of Holland's favourite Ionic columns, the central pair more widely spaced to allow better views out. Only the barely visible basement windows have any form of decoration. All this plainness was originally mitigated a little by the Harley coat of arms which once obscured the lunette window in the pediment.

The courtyard front of the house

The layout of the interior (see plan on the inside front cover) is a development of that Holland had devised for Clive of India's much larger villa at Claremont in Surrey. The principal and the smaller back stairs are set side by side in the centre of the block and so have to be illuminated from above by skylights. The principal rooms on the ground floor are laid out round them on the north, west and south sides where they enjoy the best views of the park.

Specially favoured visitors would be driven through the park to the west front, where they would climb the broad steps fronting the portico and be received at the tall round-headed front door – another very French feature. Beyond the door is the Marble Hall, where Holland's mastery of complex spatial effects becomes apparent. At first sight, the ceiling seems to be domed, but in fact the central section is a flat circle set on low arches and corner spandrels. The quality of the marble floor, the mahogany doors and the rest of the fittings is uniformly high, and suggests that Holland brought the best of his London craftsmen with him.

The style of the decoration in the Marble Hall

(Left)
A trophy of arms in the Marble Hall

(Right)
The French flagship, the 'Ville de Paris', surrenders at sunset during the Battle of the Saints in 1782: by Thomas Luny (Dining Room). The victory brought Rodney a peerage

is again indebted to contemporary French Neo-classicism, in particular the roundels over the doors, which are draped with garlands and enclose plaster trophies of arms in low relief. Similar roundels appear in the Library next door, but there they are filled with grisaille paintings of the Muses attributed to Biagio Rebecca, who had worked for Holland at Claremont and may also have provided the ceiling paintings in the Drawing Room and the Dining Room. Below the grisaille roundels in the Library, pedimented bookcases divided by delicate pilasters run round the room, like a Neo-classical temple turned inside-out.

Holland was an expert at staircases. The Staircase Hall at Berrington is the climax of the house and one of his finest surviving achievements. He dramatised an awkward space between the two sets of stairs by setting one coffered arch within another, slightly flatter, arch which supports the landing above. The staircase with its beautiful mahogany handrail and bronzed lyre-back balustrade climbs round the other three sides of the Staircase Hall to an upper landing divided by

screens of scagliola columns, arches and round-headed niches, the whole topped by a delicate domed skylight.

For Lady Sykes, who visited Berrington in 1796, these subtle effects were spoilt by the 'very offen-sive' presence of a watercloset at the top of the stairs. Holland was commissioned to provide two – with marble basins and mahogany seats. There were no separate bathrooms: Harley would have washed in his dressing-room. On the other hand, Lady Sykes thought the bedrooms, which had elegant wooden chimneypieces designed by Holland, 'convenient and comfortable'. To reduce noise, the partitions between the bedroom walls were 'partly nogined with Brick and part fill'd with sawdust'. The floor was specially thickened for the same reason, and in order to inhibit fire.

Holland also paid considerable attention to the needs of the servants. The main kitchen was in the basement, which was connected to the principal floors and to the servants' bedrooms in the attics by the back stairs. The secondary kitchen, scullery and pantry were in the north pavilion. The east pavilion

contained the laundry and bakehouse; the south pavilion the servants' hall, larder, wash-house and dairy. With its plain grey tiles and Greek key decoration in the Louis XVI style, the dairy 'was much recommended to our inspection', according to Lady Sykes:

You enter through a small room where the principal business is done. There were some good looking home made cheeses. The state apartment was furnished with two sets of china milk bowls, one of foreign coloured, the other of English blue and white.

Harley seems at first to have envisaged a fairly plain interior, with pine chimneypieces rather than marble. But his ideas were transformed by the marriage in April 1781 of his elder daughter and heir Anne to George Rodney, favourite son of Admiral Rodney. The Admiral was one of the most famous seamen of the age, but he was continually in debt, and in 1775 had had to flee to Paris to escape his creditors. Fortunately, his brother-in-law was Henry Drummond, another partner in the bank. He was also friendly with Harley, who was just as keen to encourage a match which would bring fame to Berrington and a fortune to the Rodneys. The Admiral wrote to his son in September 1780:

When you see Mr Harley, who is a very old Acquaintance, remember me to him and, my dear George, if your Heart is touched by either of his Daughters, indulge the Flame; she is of a great and noble family.

George's heart *was* touched, and during the engagement his prospects dramatically improved when the Admiral captured the island of St Eustatius in the Dutch West Indies and with it booty worth £1 million. Frustratingly, however, this windfall remained out of reach, while Rodney's political enemies challenged his right to it.

Harley had cemented his partnership with the Drummonds by marrying off his younger daughter Martha to John Drummond's son George in 1779. He celebrated these useful alliances by commissioning three-quarter-length portraits of both daughters from Gainsborough. Gainsborough also painted for him full-lengths of George and Martha Drummond and of Admiral Rodney, after his return from his final triumphant victory at the Battle of the Saints in April 1782. These once hung with Thomas Luny's

great paintings of that battle in the Dining Room, which was also given a grand marble chimneypiece carved with naval motifs as a further celebration of the Admiral's prowess. The maritime theme was continued outside where bronze cannons captured by Rodney at the so-called 'Moonlight Battle' in 1780 stood on the lawn.

THE RODNEYS

Harley remained MP for Herefordshire until 1802, apparently sharing Berrington with the young Rodneys. The Admiral was also a welcome visitor, who had his own suite on the east side of the bedroom floor overlooking the courtyard. Harley's last years were clouded by a run on the banks following an invasion scare in 1797, which seriously damaged his firm, Raymond, Harley, Webber & Co. Harley succeeded in rescuing the company and outlived his son-in-law by two years, bequeathing the estate to his grandson, another George Rodney, in 1804. The 3rd Lord Rodney seems to have been content to live quietly at Berrington, serving as Lord Lieutenant of neighbouring Radnorshire for almost 40 years. He married the sister of a Welsh magnate, the 1st Lord Tredegar, but neither he nor his two younger brothers had any children, so that when he died in 1842, the estate passed sideways in rapid succession until it was inherited by a seven-year-old grand-nephew in 1864.

The 7th Lord Rodney was to be Berrington's undoing. He was briefly a captain in the Life Guards in the 1880s, when he fought in the Egyptian campaign. In 1891 he married Corisande Guest, who was horrified by Berrington's lack of modern plumbing. Shortly after the honeymoon, a tower in rendered brick was built on to the courtyard front of the house to provide bathrooms and lavatories for the eastern range of bedrooms; it also offered spectacular views over the park from the roof, but destroyed the house's delicate symmetry.

The Rodneys rapidly produced an heir, but the marriage turned sour. The 4,000-acre estate had never recovered from the agricultural depression of the 1870s, and the gambling debts the 7th Baron ran up on the turf only made matters worse. With grim

The elaborate marble chimneypiece in the Dining Room seems to refer to Admiral Rodney's naval prowess. This panel includes Britannia's shield and trident

Sarah, Lady Rodney (wife of the 6th Lord Rodney) lived at Berrington in the mid-19th century; by Sir Francis Grant (property of Edward Harley Esq.)

symbolism, the stable block caught fire and was left a burnt-out ruin. To raise cash, the Gainsboroughs were sold in the 1880s. The shelves of the Library were emptied, and it was turned into a billiard-room. More and more went, until finally in 1901 he was forced to dispose of the house and the estate. The following year his wife divorced him.

THE CAWLEYS

In 1901, the year the Rodneys left Berrington, Queen Victoria died. The country went into mourning, and the demand for black crêpe soared. This was good news for the man who bought Berrington that year, Frederick Cawley. For he owned the patent for a pure black dye which made his cotton-finishing business one of the most successful in Lancashire.

Frederick Cawley's career mirrors that of Thomas Harley in several ways. He was a younger son, indeed the youngest of the six sons of Thomas Cawley, who was agent to John, later Lord, Tollemache at Peckforton Castle, a gigantic neo-medieval country house in Cheshire built by Anthony Salvin between 1844 and 1850, the year Frederick was born. At the age of seventeen he was sent as an apprentice to J. & N. Philips, one of the great dynasties of Manchester merchants, whose various branches built large houses in Radnorshire, Kent and Warwickshire, as well as in Prestwich to the north of Manchester. Cawley learnt quickly and married wisely, going into partnership with his brother-in-law and soon taking control of their cotton-finishing business, which became the Heaton Mills Bleaching Company. Around 1890 he was elected a councillor on the Manchester Corporation, and in 1895 Liberal MP for the Prestwich division of Lancashire. By the turn of the century he had the wealth and the social position to support not one, but two Georgian country houses.

Cawley moved from Moss House beside his factory to Brooklands, a plain early 18th-century villa near Heaton Park, which came with eleven acres of grounds, an increasingly rare commodity as the suburbs of Manchester expanded north-wards. At the same time he bought Berrington as a country retreat from Westminster and his constituency; it was then well-served by the railway station at Berrington & Eye.

At first the Herefordshire gentry did not take kindly to their new neighbour: not only was he in trade, but a 'damn radical' to boot (Thomas Harley and the Rodneys had all been Tories). Soon after Cawley arrived, he replaced the decayed honey-suckle frieze on the pediment with an acanthus design. Around 1908 he began a comprehensive but sensitive redecoration of the interior. He replaced ugly Victorian tiled fireplaces with more appropriate 18th-century steel grates, including, most spectacularly, that embellished with Wedgwood plaques in the Drawing Room. He also put up Aubusson tapestries in the Marble and Staircase Halls to fill the gaps left by the naval pictures the Rodneys had sold. The house was converted to electricity supplied by a generator in the Dairy, and the eastern range of the service block was turned into new stables, where he bred racehorses.

(Above) One of the Aubosson-Felletin tapestry panels commissioned by the 1st Lord Cawley

The most successful was Formidable, named after Admiral Rodney's flagship at the Battle of the Saints.

For his services to the Liberal Party in the north-west, Cawley was made a baronet in 1906. Appropriately for a Lancashire MP, he was Chancellor of the Duchy of Lancaster in Lloyd George's wartime coalition government, retiring from the Commons with a peerage in 1918. This was little consolation for the grievous losses he suffered in the Great War. His third son, Stephen, a brilliant young staff officer in the 1st Cavalry Brigade, was killed at Nery during the retreat from Mons in 1914. His second son, Harold, died at Gallipoli the following year. Cawley subsequently served on the commission of inquiry into the Dardanelles fiasco, which published a letter from Harold Cawley bitterly criticising the conduct of the campaign. And then in August 1918, three months from the end of the war, his youngest son, Oswald, died at Merville on the Western Front.

Lord Cawley's wife Elizabeth never really recovered from this triple blow. Their grandson,

the 3rd Lord Cawley, remembered her as a kind, but rather formidable woman who devoted her life to Berrington, running the large household with Victorian formality. Children were not allowed to use the main stairs or to tamper with the wireless in the Library. Her principal relaxations were Mah-Jong and needlework, of which fine examples can be seen in the Boudoir. The staff were ruled by Williams the butler, 'a monumental figure, kindly and immensely pompous', who taught the young Frederick Cawley to fish in the pool in 1919.

The Cawleys' eldest and only surviving son, Robert, married Vivienne Lee, from another leading Lancashire cotton family, who were partners in Tootal Broadhurst Lee. He moved into Brooklands in 1918, when his parents retired to Berrington, and moved here in 1937 on his father's death. The 2nd Lord Cawley brought a more informal regime. He introduced mains electric lighting and began renovating the attics and basement, but before work could start on the main rooms, war broke out. The Cawleys suffered once again. Their youngest son, John, was killed at Tunis in 1943, and their eldest, Frederick, wounded during the fierce tank battles of the Normandy campaign in 1944.

45

(Above) The ugly water-tower was added to the courtyard façade in the late 19th century and demolished in the 1960s, when it was found to be riddled with dry-rot

Berrington itself came through unscathed. It was used as a convalescent hospital, run from her office in the Boudoir by Lady Cawley, who was much involved in the British Red Cross and the National Council of Women. In the run-up to the Normandy landings, a brigade of American troops was stationed in the park; the concrete footings of their huts still survive.

THE NATIONAL TRUST

When the 2nd Lord Cawley died in 1954, Berrington was handed over in part-payment of death-duties to the Treasury, which transferred it to the National Trust. The 3rd Lord Cawley had been brought up at Brooklands, and after he was called to the Bar in 1938, he needed a home nearer London. However, his mother, Vivienne, Lady Cawley, who had generously endowed the property, continued to live at Berrington until her death in 1978 at the age of 100.

In 1796 Lady Sykes had thought Berrington 'very ill executed, being very much cracked'. By the mid-1960s the soft sandstone with which the house was faced had become seriously decayed, especially where it was exposed to the prevailing south-west winds. It was decided to replace the worst affected areas with a similar-coloured, but more durable, red Hollington sandstone quarried near Uttoxeter. When the ugly bathroom tower was also found to be riddled with dry-rot, it was taken down, and the pediment over the courtyard façade reinstated. However, the steps and the off-centre entrance door were retained, so that Lady Cawley could continue to enjoy her sitting-room. The work took from 1966 until 1970 and was made possible thanks to substantial grant-aid from the Historic Buildings Council.

BIBLIOGRAPHY

BAKER, Norman, *Government and Contractors: The British Treasury and War Supplies 1775–1783*, London, 1971.

BOLITHO, Hector, and Derek Peel, *The Drummonds of Charing Cross*, London, 1967.

CORNFORTH, John, 'Berrington Hall, Herefordshire', *Country Life*, 9 January 1992, pp. 42–5.

DORMENT, Richard, *British Painting in the Philadelphia Museum of Art*, London, 1986, pp. 128–30.

HUSSEY, Christopher, *English Country Houses: Mid Georgian*, London, 1956, pp. 184–94.

LOVELL, Mary S., *A Scandalous Life: The Biography of Jane Digby el Mezrab*, London, 1995.

RUDÉ, George, *Wilkes and Liberty*, Oxford, 1962.

SPINNEY, David, *Rodney*, London, 1969.

STROUD, Dorothy, *Henry Holland*, London, 1966.

STROUD, Dorothy, *Capability Brown*, London, 1975.

The west front

THE NATIONAL TRUST

for Places of Historic Interest or Natural Beauty

This guide describes one of the many historic or beautiful places protected by the National Trust in England, Wales and Northern Ireland.

The National Trust was founded in 1895 by three visionary Victorians to acquire and hold places of historic interest or natural beauty for the benefit of the nation.

It is now one of Europe's leading conservation charities, supported by more than 2.9 million subscribing members, as well as legacies, bequests and donations. Each year over 40,000 volunteers make an invaluable contribution to the Trust's continuing work.

You can help

The National Trust needs your support, and is immensely grateful to all those who make a contribution to its work.

You can help by:

– becoming a subscribing member

– considering a legacy (see right)

– making a donation

– if already a member, joining an Association of members

– making a gift of your time, energy, skills and enthusiasm as a volunteer.

For more details contact the National Trust Membership Department, PO Box 39, Warrington WA5 7WD or telephone 0844 800 1895 (minicom 0844 800 4410) e.mail enquiries@thenationaltrust.org.uk or see our website at: www.nationaltrust.org.uk.

Legacies

Have you ever considered leaving a charitable bequest in your Will? Whatever their size, legacies are vital to the National Trust. They are the second largest source of income for the Trust, and we could not survive without them. They are used to fund major restoration projects, to acquire and endow new properties around the country, or for any other area of the Trust's work that you may wish to specify. **They are not spent on administration costs**.

Remembering the National Trust with a legacy may also prevent your estate from paying Inheritance Tax and will at the same time help to maintain the special heritage of England, Wales and Northern Ireland for future generations.

A free booklet is available providing helpful advice on will-making in general, as well as suggested wording, should you wish to support the National Trust in some way.

For your copy or for further information, please contact the Legacies Department, The National Trust, Heelis, Kemble Drive, Swindon, Wilts SN2 2NA; telephone 01793 817685/01793 817505 e.mail: enquiries@thenationaltrust.org.uk.